MYTHS & MONSTERS

OF RESTON, VIRGINIA

THE PHENOMENAL AND FRIGHTENING FINDINGS OF
DR. PADRAIGIN W. THALMEUS, PDS.

BY ERIC MACDICKEN
& KRISTINA S. ALCORN

The truth may be out there!
— Kristina

EVERY JOURNEY BEGINS WITH A SINGLE STEP. ENJOY!
— Eric

First edition.

Great Owl Books
GreatOwlBooks.com

Design and Illustrations:
© Eric MacDicken

Cover photos:
© Caroline Schor-MacDicken

Author photos:
Courtesy of Kristina S. Alcorn
Courtesy of Eric MacDicken

Great Owl Books
GreatOwlBooks.com
"You Are What You Read"

Visit
MYTHSandMONSTERSorRESTON.com

GREAT OWL
Great Owl Books

For the pure love of books.

Acknowledgements

Many thanks for illumination and inspiration:
Mike Mignola, Guillermo del Toro, Douglas Adams, John Tenniel, E.H. Shepard, Willis O'Brien, Ub Iwerks, Mary Blair, Washington Irving, Mary Shelley, King Tutankhamun, Jane Goodall, Josh Gates, Amy Poehler, Dr. Henry Jones Jr., The Gill-man, *Weekly World News*, and the spectacular country of Scotland.

Many thanks for encouragement and boundless support:
Brian, Mark, Sandy, Arnold and Greta, Dr. Ray, Susie K, Jake, Chloe, Caitlin, Carolyn and Matt, Gigi and Todd. And my immense gratitude to Kristina—an exceptional storyteller, writer, humorist, and dear friend. And, of course, my undying appreciation and admiration to my very own mythical muse, Caroline.

— *Eric*

First and foremost, I must thank Bob Simon for making this book possible. For without Bob, there is no Reston. And that alone is a scary thought. Fortunately for us, Bob had the vision and tenacity to turn 6,750 acres of farmland into a community we get to call home. While working on the book *In His Own Words*, Eric and I pondered the myths swirling around Bob (most amusingly that he was an oil-rich playboy creating a hippy utopia) and the more fantastical ones we recalled from our Reston childhoods (most notably The Bunny Man and The Nudist Colony). We lamented the dearth of Reston-inspired myths and legends, and seized the opportunity to explore what might be in the woods and lakes around us—if we only took a closer look.

Secondly, without Eric's encyclopedia knowledge of mythology, staggering artistic talent, unfettered imagination, and apparent disdain for sleep, we'd still be talking about these myths rather than enjoying them on the pages that follow. I treasured this opportunity to collaborate once again.

And last but not least, I'd like to thank my family for their support while I was away on fact-finding expeditions for this book. The truth (or something like it) is out there—thanks for holding down the fort while I looked.

— *Kristina*

Introduction

When we are not busy finding ways to keep a roof over our heads and food in our bellies, human beings go in search of stories. Even at night, while our bodies sleep, our minds stitch scraps of tales into magical quilts to keep us warm. And at the heart of storytelling live the myths we create and share, one person to another, one generation to the next, each retelling adding new layers and colors to the tales. Myths explain the inexplicable; they give us meaning and purpose; they bind us to one another. The heroes and creatures of myths are as essential to our survival as the fires we light against the dark and cold.

– Gigi Thibodeau
writer and Adjunct Professor of English,
University of Massachusetts Lowell

Myths & Monsters will take you on a fun-filled romp through adventure and fantasy, inspired by the natural places that weave through our community. Ripe for exploration and best enjoyed with a sense of wonder, MacDicken and Alcorn encourage new generations to get outside, search for critters, peek into hiding places, and let their imaginations soar. Those of us who grew up in Reston will love the humor contained in this wild tale, plus the challenge of dissecting fact and fiction.

– Katie Shaw
Walker Nature Center Manager
Restonian since 1968

Forward
from the
Research Team

While conducting research for a book on the history of Reston, the Emerald Jewel of Northern Virginia, our team delved through countless volumes of historic documents, chronolographs, municipal records, and archived newspapers... that's when we made a discovery of unprecedented importance.

On one of our many fact-finding trips to the Reston Regional Library, a particular custodian of the athenaeum (who has asked to remain anonymous) alluded to the existence of a confidential and well-hidden vault of uncatalogued books.

We were given permission to peruse the secret room and discovered among the clutter a tattered book of mysterious origin. Our librarian guide relayed that it was believed to have been unearthed in the red clay banks of a South Reston watershed by construction workers while digging a site for a new office building—or perhaps townhouses. Either way, the book was turned over to the library's Director of Obscure Texts and Opuscule Oddities, who surreptitiously stowed it in the vault.

The thick volume of molding parchment pages was bound in a dark-brown leather cover, embossed with the words:
> *Myths & Monsters of the Lower Patowmack*
> *and Greater Falls. Virginia*

And on the first decaying page was handwritten in faded ink:
> *Dr. Padraigin W. Thalmeus, PDS.*
> *1819*

The following are pages directly from Dr. Thalmeus' journal, paired with the findings of our research team.

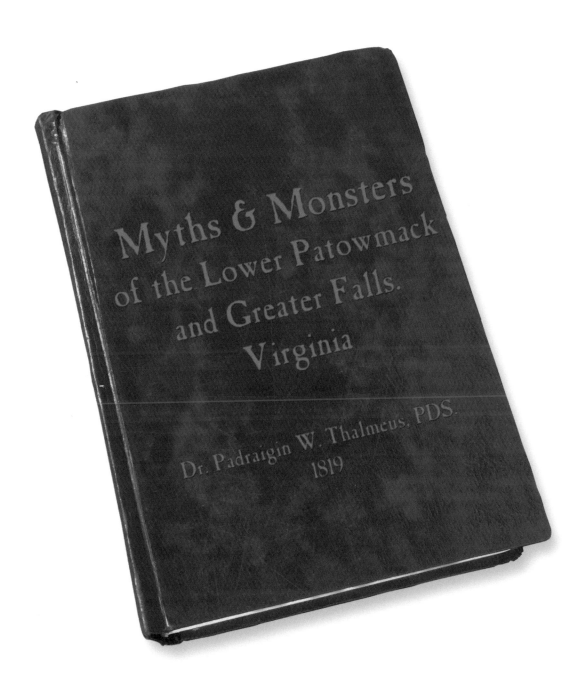

Day 1, October 19, 7pm
Confounded Curse! My guide and porter have deserted me. Yes, we did hear what can only be the agonized wailing of a disembodied vaporous wraith. True, it followed us without pause until we were exhausted to near hysteria... but who can say it was truly the Bollin Banshee?!

It was she who lured me here in the first place and condemns me to my present pitiful condition. How I wish I'd never shared that dram of sherry with Sir Frairdecodd. He further intoxicated me with the tale of his 13th failed expedition to Virginia in search of the Bollin Banshee's treasure of incalculable wealth. That is what spirited me on this venture: the gold and jewels of Eight Thousand Cursed Souls. I'm alone, lost, abandoned... but oh, what a find that will be! I shall carry on alone. – D.W.T.

Historical Research

Our team's first undertaking was tracking down the history of both Dr. Thalmeus,[1] and Sir Rechmounth Frairdecodd, Esq., whom Thalmeus mentions on this page of his field guide journal. It appears Sir Frairdecodd was a fortune-seeker of some note who often bragged in London pubs of his conquests, but was suspiciously always broke.
He completely disappears from any accounts by 1819, the same year Dr. Thalmeus wrote his journal.
We knew we had to know more.

Sir Renchmounth Frairdecodd, Esq.
(or perhaps a descendant)

The Bollin Banshee

THE BOLLIN BANSHEE

Exhaustive research led us to the back stacks of Reston's Used Book Store and a book of rare supernatural occurrences, titled *Rare Supernatural Occurrences*, by Janet Feldworts, PhD., c1929. In Dr. Feldworts' tome, she describes a wailing phantom woman "of mystery and mist" who may have once been Lady Katherine Bollin, the eminent English psychic.[2] Lady Katherine was a fierce critic of those who sought to plunder faraway lands, often quoted saying, "Diamonds are a poor best friend. They can't even play Bridge."

Some credit her avenging spirit with centuries of shipwrecks off America's east coast and the disappearance of the ill-gotten gains they carried. Even now, on moonlit nights on the golf courses of Reston, you can hear her banshee wail guarding the "Treasure of Eight Thousand Cursed Souls."

Day 2, October 20, 6am

The Bollin Banshee is no myth! Last eve the vaporous vexation chased me across hill and moor, driving me into the woods, where the wailing faded into the night. I stumbled through the dark until I found a path wide enough for a carriage and promptly stubbed my toe on an oversized horseshoe. Just as I reached for the offending object, an arrow sliced through the night, narrowly missing my noggin before smashing a nearby tree trunk to splinters. Rearing above me was a mighty horse darker than midnight, whose rider wielded a brutal crossbow, and to my dismay the huntsman had no head! I ran as though shot from a cannon before I fell heel over head into a ravine and out cold.

THE RECKLESS HUNTSMAN

This myth bears some resemblance to another well-known Horseman, famous for riding his frightful steed each Halloween night through the deep woods, on a quest to swap his Jack-O-Lantern for a human head. Given the family resemblance, these two must be brothers. But Reston's Reckless Huntsman is often reported by those unlucky enough to see him as being a bit clumsy and having questionable aim with his crossbow.

Unsubstantiated reports claim the original settlers called this area
"The Haunter's Woods'" which was misunderstood by travellers as "Hunters Woods."

Day 2, October 20, 5pm
Nestled behind a towering hedge this eve as the sun set,
I happened upon a village scene of near complete normalcy
– gentlemen smoking pipes, ladies strolling, cobblers
cobbling. But for their outright lack of clothing, save for
shoes and hats, and their obvious contentment,
I could have mistaken this locale
for my own town back in Europe.
Enticed, and admittedly lonely,
I wondered how, pray tell,
if, I could join them.
I pondered, I fled, I returned.
"Oh, balderdash!" I exclaimed,
"when in Virginia..." and
I committed to join them,
my humility in check.
I had gotten no further
than rolling down my stockings
when a creature most heinous swooped down
and plucked up a naked farmer. It faltered momentarily,
dragged down by his portliness, but rallied and winged
him away. Oh, the horrors of this cursed place.

ENGLAND 3600 Miles

THE RESTON NUDIST COLONY

Despite raids from supernatural beings, locust plagues, incurable rashes, snakebites, dysentery, typhoid, cholera, and generalized exhaustion, this secluded spot continued to attract nudist settlers for hundreds of years.

Primitive woodcuts discovered by archaeologists from the prestigious University of Epidermisology shed light on the quotidian activities of Colonial-era nudies. "These *Naked Quakers* as I like to call them, were a group of highly resourceful nudists with a fastidious devotion to their head and footwear," explained ethnonudobotinist, Dr. Seymour Keister. The last descendents of the group remained in the enclave until the early 1960's when Reston's developers invited them to "...get dressed or get out."

To this day, Reston teens caught skinny-dipping have reported seeing ghosts "wearing nothing but funny hats" in Lake Audubon, near the former settlement.

Some nudist purists argue that you cannot truly be considered a nudist if you are sporting a hat and shoes.

Day 3, October 21, 7am
Before he ran off that first day, my cowardly guide ominously plucked insect shells the size of my largest toe from tree limbs, calling them "cicadas." As the dry husks disintegrated in his trembling hand, he foretold of a great plague: the land-covering, sky-choking, 13-year swarm was close at hand. He claimed they travelled in numbers great enough to carry off a man! But this is not what I observed last night! Instead, I witnessed with my own eyes a 9-foot tall, regally dressed and pompadoured cicada-woman flying overhead with the unconscious nudist in her clutches. I followed her through the forest to a clearing, where she landed. Her glimmering orange eyes sliced through the fog and illuminated a circle of small mounds of earth. I watched in horror as she burrowed a hole the size of a man's body. Her frenetic digging came to a dead stop as she raised her gaze to meet mine. I fled before she could add me to her collection!

THE CICADA LADY

AKA *The Lady Cicada* was last sighted in 1978 when a prank went horribly wrong. Seven Herndon High School students ventured deep into the woods, eager to capture and display her alongside their Herndon Hornet mascot at Homecoming. While the boys were never seen again, investigators found Polaraid photos documenting their hunt scattered on the forest ground. The most haunting image appeared to be one enormous orange eye.

Cicadas still descend upon, or rather *ascend* upon (since they actually emerge from underground), the region every 7, 13, and 17 years; however, the decline of the nudist population seems to have lead to the extinction of the gigantic, man-eating variety.

The cicada "song" has been described by acoustic experts as "deafening timbal clicks."

"The Lady Cicada"

Day 3, October 21, 5pm

Well, that was simply unpleasant.

I stepped in something squishy, possibly the letter "T" formed from mud. I found a similarly fashioned "R" then "O" and possibly two "L"s. A terrible, unearthly smell followed me. As the world-renowned scat tracker Prenteth Boundshauph says: "If it looks, feels, and smells like poop, it probably is." I banged my soiled shoe against a large tree and in doing so roused an angry Tree Hole Troll. He jutted his head through the hole and menacingly brandished an ambivalent frog dangling on a fishing line. "None mayeth passeth, lest ye payeth the toll!" he belched at me.

"Toll? How much?" I asked.

"A tooshurence."

"That's highway robbery! Oh, fine. What should I expect from a troll. Well, do you have change for a bobbender?"

"Hold on a sec," he snorted, then squeezed his ample rump through the tree hole and emerged counting coins in his pudgy little hands.

"Now jog on, Prattler! 'Fore I change my mind!"

TREE HOLE TROLL

Of course, it is a well known fact that Trolls collect tolls, and have throughout history in myths and fables from around the world. Competing versions of this particular Troll have him living in different places, even under Lake Anne's Van Gogh Bridge. Despite location, the fee to cross in the stories is usually a "tooshurence"—Olde English slang like 'ha'penny' or 'tuppence'—leading historians to believe the Reston Tree Hole Troll was of either English or Irish origin. A tooshurence, adjusted for inflation and exchange rates, is about $19.64, or roughly the current cost of travelling the Dulles Toll Road one way. In some tellings, the Tree Hole Troll is guarding the Bollin Banshee's Treasure of Eight Thousand Cursed Souls.

His footprints, men's size 17, are often found alongside bicycle paths near the Walker Nature Center. For you trackers out there, these prints are not to be confused with Big-Toe's, which stand out due to the, well, big toes.

Many have said that you can track the Tree Hole Troll by the distinctive alphabet scat.

Day 5, October 23, 7pm

This was a day I will long wish to forget!

While following the poor excuse for a map left to me by my guide, I found the oddest of tracks. Footprints like those of a man, but here you think me mad. The pinky toe on both feet was the size of a billiard ball! While pondering this anomaly, I was pelted about the face and eyes by acorns! I heard a snickering, wheezy laughter coming from a nearby shrub and looked up to see a hairy beast, sauntering off into the woods with a wide gait, dropping acorns as he went. After a moment I thought it safe to venture onward again, when I was knocked unconscious! I awoke hours later covered in acorns, my face swollen with acorn welts. What could I do? I resigned myself to make acorn stew.

BIG-TOE

Sasquatch, Bigfoot, Yeti, Chewbacca, the Abominable Snowman...
by any name, the legendary hairy behemoth has left his indelible
foot-print on the imaginations of believers, skeptics, and campers all
over the globe.

If you're walking on a Reston path alone, and you hear an acorn fall
nearby, or are clunked on the head by one, you have undoubtedly
just had an encounter with Big-Toe.
Big-Toe Strikes Again!

Day 8, October 26, 8am

Last night was a dreadful nightmare.

After eluding the hirsute harasser, I tripped headlong into wretched bogginess along the railroad tracks and rested at the foot of a gnarled tree. When the glow of a hundred fireflies illuminated its viney toes kneading the mud, I instantly recognized my mistake. My gaze slowly raised to take in the measure of the being. This was not botanical, rather a creature I can best describe as half man, half swamp colossus – wearing a jaunty tricorn hat. Zounds!

Overcome by fright (or perhaps his odor), I passed out cold.

I awoke this this morning at my own camp and sitting beside me was a whiskey neat.

THE VIRGINIA SWAMPMAN (aka *Swamp Man*)

The *Legend of the Virginia Swampman* has stayed alive for generations through vivid imaginations and traditional oral history. But few know that his image was actually captured on an early 19th century liquor bottle, proudly serving his distilled concoction. The swamp of yesteryear described by Dr. Thalmeus is now a lily pad-filled lake around which runners and cyclists enjoying the W&OD trail stop to catch their breath. On warm autumn evenings, when you see groups of fireflies hovering around the pond, Restonians know the *Virginia Swampman* is close at hand.

The "Virginia Swamp Man" bourbon label

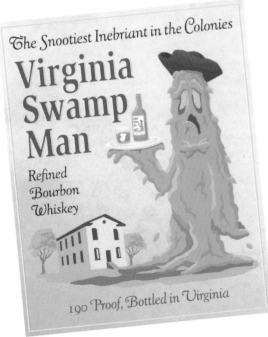

If you hope to spot him, keep an eye out for large groups of fireflies.

Day 9, October 27, 5am
Eerie clanging and tortured mumbling awoke me from a fretful slumber. A not-quite human voice slowly repeated "moost eet grrrainns" in a chorus with others. Looking through the early morning fog, I rubbed the sleep from my eyes to be sure what I was seeing; a hundred dairy cows advancing toward me, dragging their hoofs. Their deadened eyes, glowing like cold, pale moonlight. I ran till breathless, sure to find them at my heels. They'd made no progress but stared on. I approached the leader, sure to keep clear of his mighty chompers, then briskly tipped him over, unintentionally toppling the entire herd like a line of dominos. Then I ran more.

ZOMBIE COWS

Our team dug deep to find the earliest report of Zombie Cows in early America. One researcher turned in her findings[3] then quit over the matter, saying, "Cows are too often maligned and treated disrespectfully. This is bogus. I'm out of here." The end of her report included: "Cows are much smarter than people want to believe. They do have feelings and they care lovingly for their young." So we extend our sincere apologies to all *Non-Zombie Cows*, but Zombie Cows creeped out Dr. Thalmeus in his journal, so we must conclude that they are real and surely still exist on farms throughout the world. Lacking evidence to the contrary, there really is no other logical conclusion.

moost eet grrraainnns

The next time you hear a clang of the undead cowbell, run! (Or at least walk quickly)

Day 9, October 27, 5am

Of all the consternations I have encountered on this ill-fated treasure hunt, nothing prepared me for the graceful creature I shall call Annie, for she reminds me of my third-cousin, twice-removed, on my Uncle Bhàtair's side of the family. With childlike wonder, I spied Annie gliding effortlessly through the moonlit lake then disappear below the surface. The tranquility that enveloped the lakeshore was soon shattered by an enormous torrent, 300 feet high, emerging from the dragon's spout.

It rivaled the fountains of Florence or Versailles.

ANNIE, THE LAKE ANNE MONSTER

Hardly a *monster* in the traditional sense, this gentle, majestic matriarch of myth has relatives in *every* major body of water—Nessie (Loch Ness), Chessie (Chesapeake Bay), Champ (Lake Champlain), Ogopogo (Okanagan Lake), Lusca, Aspidochelone, Jörmungandr, the Kraken...

It stands to reason that if you live near water, you live near a "sea monster."

When you see bubbles rising to the surface of Lake Anne, you can be sure that you just saw Annie.

Scientists recently discovered that the Greenland shark can live up to 500 years, and who's to say Annie isn't a relative. Given that, Annie must be quite young for a sea serpent, so we can look forward to seeing her in Lake Anne for centuries to come.

Day 10, October 28, 8am
I awoke hoping to see Annie in the glistening lake,
but to my astonishment I have finally found treasure!
Callootenay! Perhaps not the Treasure of Eight
Thousand Cursed Souls, but the gold and jewels of
the Egyptian Pharaohs! Before me protruding from
the dirt are the tops of stone pyramids! At last, my
fortune awaits only my digging!

Day 12, October 30, 3pm
After a three day excavation I have unearthed bizarre
structures that could not possibly have been made by
human hands. No gold. No rubies. No emeralds.
I shall have very terse words for Sir Frairdecodd.

ANCIENT ALIEN CIVILIZATION

It is widely believed that visiting architects from distant planets, and possibly other dimensions, built the mysterious Stonehenge, the pyramids of Egypt, the great cities of the Mayans, and the products of Apple.

There is indisputable evidence of this in Reston, with the other-worldly stone structures and sculptures[4] in and around Lake Anne Plaza.

Over the decades, Reston has been a popular destination of thousands of truth-seekers (including the popular 1970's *In Search Of…* television show) yearning to discover proof of extraterrestrial artisans, the remains of their ancient civilization, and perhaps interplanetary communications.

Day 13, October 31, 4pm
I discovered what I believe
to be an encrypted language
on the alien structures
and have followed
those clues north.
Unable to find any
paths or hints of humanity, and finding the thick forest
impassable, I was forced to wade through a stream bed.
This treasure hunt has become my bane. I know it is out
there, calling to me—but my back aches, my eyes burn, my
stomach groans. Riches will cure these ailments.
Upon noon, I nearly took for a log this critter, which
slowly crawled out to greet me. It is not dissimilar to a
dog, with the lustrous skin of a slug. Or salamander?
Unlike many of the other encounters on this journey, this
bloke seems to enjoy following me making guttural grunts,
as if passing gas from its mouth. It seems benign, but
mostly I find it to be a pest. I have taught it to play fetch,
in hopes it would get lost in the thicket, but it continues
to return with jubilance. Perhaps if I do not find food
or treasure soon I will make a meal of it.

SLUG DOG GILAMANDER

As the Virginia Colony was home to many Scottish and Irish immigrants, surely this remarkable creature stowed away aboard a vessel for the New World, and found its way to this New Town. The Dobhar-chú, as it is known in Gaelic folklore, is a monstrous water hound—part dog, part Hellbender salamander—that fishermen on Lake Newport blame for taking only their biggest catches.

These elusive creatures—who hide in streams, watersheds, and lakes—have been reported to animal control as recently as 2009. Their diet consists of crickets and cicadas.

The cryptozoology journal *Xtremophiled* asserts that the Slug Dog Gilamander is a mutated Giant Otter of the Amazon; the rather frightening cousin of the cute and fluffy River and Sea Otters. Giant Otters weigh up to 70 pounds, have imposing fangs, protruding eyes, and startling dining manners. They are so fearless that even caiman (the alligatorid crocodilian) are on the menu. Needless to say, this cousin is not often invited to the Fluffy Family reunions.

Day 13, October 31, 10pm
The Bollin Banshee can have her treasure! All I want
is safe passage out of this land of vicious supernatural
abominations! I found what I believe to be train tracks.
Time to make my escape! But that pesky Slug Dog
came back for another game of fetch. At least I thought
it was that harmless compatriot. What emerged from the
bushes was far from friendly.

This demon on eight legs has eyes that burn like coal
embers, fire bursting from its throat, black smoke spewing
from its nostrils. Followed by two more of its rapacious
brethren, the trio sprang toward me like a locomotive,
roaring relentlessly to overtake me. The ferocious
Choochoocabra chased me up a tree where I am still!

CHOOCHOOCABRA

While there is no evidence that Dr. Thalmeus was familiar with Spanish language and folklore, his name for this creature bears a close resemblance to another well-known monster, the Chupacabra (Spanish for "goat sucker"). Given that Choochoocabra loosely translates to "goat train," our research team is willing to bet this is mere coincidence.

Contemporary encounters date as recently as 1986, when a group of South Lakes High School graduates told authorities they were "chased on the W&OD Trail[5] from Old Reston Avenue to Isaac Newton Square" by three dog-like creatures with "like, way too many legs, day-glow-orange eyes, and smoke blasting from their noses."

The incident was largely dismissed by officials, saying the teens likely saw frisky raccoons or playful beavers.

Courtesy of **Xtremophiled**: The Definitive Journal of Cryptozoology

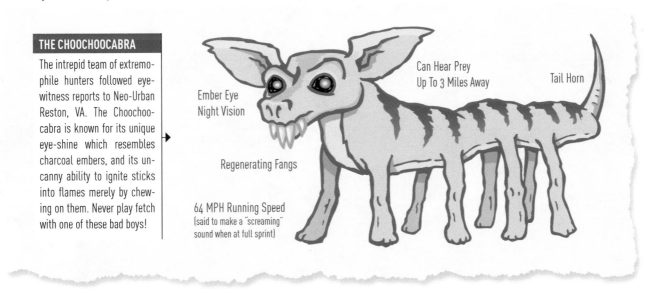

THE CHOOCHOOCABRA

The intrepid team of extremophile hunters followed eyewitness reports to Neo-Urban Reston, VA. The Choochoocabra is known for its unique eye-shine which resembles charcoal embers, and its uncanny ability to ignite sticks into flames merely by chewing on them. Never play fetch with one of these bad boys!

Ember Eye
Night Vision

Regenerating Fangs

64 MPH Running Speed
(said to make a "screaming"
sound when at full sprint)

Can Hear Prey
Up To 3 Miles Away

Tail Horn

Many handwriting experts claim Dr. Thalmeus actually wrote "Choochoocobra" — meaning 'snake train.'

Day 13, October 31, 11:59pm
Something has frightened away the pack of Choochoocabra.
The something is below me now. Methodically circling
the base of the tree I am presently ensconced within the
branches of. Dimly lit by a candled lantern, I see the fiend
is... if I survive to tell the tale no one will ever believe...
it is a rabbit, the size of a man, walking on hind legs.
Carrying the lantern in one paw and a gleaming
battle axe in the other. I must be quiet while I make
this rendering of it.
I wouldn't want to...
OH NO!
It stopped!
It's slowly
turning around.
Does it see me?
It sees me!
I

THE BUNNY MAN

This was the last weather-worn page from the strange and fascinating field journal of the fastidious Dr. Padraigin W. Thalmeus, PDS. Scholars, paranormal researchers, and historical investigators all agree that his final encounter was with none other than the Bunny Man.

Some reports claim Dr. Thalmeus escaped and became an oyster farmer. Others say he was never heard from again. The truth, like the Treasure of Eight Thousand Cursed Souls, is still out there— waiting to be discovered.

"Several localities claim the Bunny Man as their own and each adds a sprinkle of local flavor. The common thread is an agitated, possibly murderous, axe- (sometimes hatchet) wielding man dressed in a bunny suit. Whether he is an escaped convict or a furry protestor of encroaching residential development, for decades local teens* have recounted surviving late night excursions to the Bunny Man Bridge (Fairfax Station) or the Bunny Man House (Reston). Since the first sightings in the early 1970s, the legend has inspired a sub-genre of Bunny Man-inspired artwork, literature, and even a rock musical by the band Mantua Finials."

From *In His Own Words: Stories from the Extraordinary Life of Reston's Founder, Robert E. Simon, Jr.*
—by Kristina S. Alcorn, Great Owl Books. *Used with permission from the author.*

Many stories include the Bunny Man skulking after meddling teens on Halloween.

Monster Map of Reston

Myths & Monsters
of the Lower Patowmack
and Greater Falls, Virginia

Dr. Padraigin W. Thalmeus, PDS.
1819

Lord Fairfax's County

Trade Route Seven

Slug Dog

Zombie Cows

Annie

Ancient City

Big-Toe

The Virginia Swampman

Troll Road

Choochoocabra

The Bunny Man

Cicada Lady

Tree Hole Troll

Bollin Banshee

The Reckless Huntsman

Haunters Woods

Oh my! Nudies!

But where is the cursed Treasure of Eight Thousand Cursed Souls?!

Lord Fairfax's County

Activity Page

Nature is AWESOME. When you venture out to find Big-Toe or the Slug Dog Gilamander, enjoy discovering the many natural wonders all around you on Reston's paths, trails, and waterways! Here are some fun things you can do in your own great outdoors... whether you live in Reston or somewhere else!

1. CREATE your own monster or myth that celebrates your town and its connection to nature. What kind of wondrous creature would live near you?

2. MAKE a map of the paths in your town where you think mythical creatures and monsters might roam. What stories can you imagine about them?

3. CAMP in your backyard, porch, deck or living room, and listen to nature at night on an after-dark adventure with friends and family. What nocturnal animal sounds can be heard?

4. EXPLORE the paths and trails near your home on your nature walks. What interesting plants and trees grow there? What nests or other habitats do you see where animals might live?

5. OBSERVE the animals during your hikes. How many animals did you see, and what species are unique to where you live?

6. CREATE a journal or diary of exploring nature in your community, adding notes or drawings, or both. Share your experiences with a friend!

7. FIND an acorn, footprints, a cicada, a feather, or a brightly colored leaf, and try looking at them under a magnifying glass. What details do you notice up close that you didn't see before?

8. GO on a day hike at your town's nearest nature park or on its local trails and bring a plant identification book or field guide. What plant life is unique to where you live?

9. HELP by volunteering for a watershed cleanup to protect the streams, ponds, lakes, rivers, and oceans and all the amazing creatures that call them home. Where is your closest watershed?

10. GET outside whenever you can and enjoy being a part of nature!

And remember, the heartiest explorers always follow these guidelines:
Respect nature and all its splendorous gifts. Stay on marked paths and trails.
Be careful not to disturb wildlife or their homes. Place rubbish in trash
cans or recycling bins. Carry-out-what-you-carry-in.
Have fun!

Appendix

1.   While our researchers did not find authentication specifically of Dr. Padraigin W. Thalmeus, PDS., there was a Dr. P.W. Thallmaus at the University of Greifswald around 1815. Not much is known about him except his department: Occult History and Ancient Grotesqueries.

　　We also found a Dr. Patrick T. Thaelmass at the Lichtenstein Community College around 1812; his writings were published in an anthology titled, *Beasts of Yore, Magick, and Night Terrors* (roughly translated).

　　Some experts we showed the journal to suggested it may be a forgery; likely created by book collector and renowned braggart Jacob H. Brandini (1837-1901; a New York socialite who hosted *de rigueur* séance parties) to win a bet with his gentlemen's club on who could find the strangest book on the occult.

　　We sought to have the journal authenticated through carbon-dating by the United States Geological Survey (USGS) in Reston, but the book went missing. Presumably stolen and sold to a private collector, or confiscated by the government to cover up the truth, we will never know the complete details.

　　Luckily, we were able to copy and transcribe most of the hundreds of pages from the journal before we gave it to the USGS; the section concerning Reston was merely the final chapter of Dr. Thalmeus' misadventures. It should be noted that many pages had clearly been torn from the journal, or were too worn to transcribe without some conjecturing.

2.   In her book, Dr. Feldworts makes a compelling case that Lady Katherine Bollin is the Bollin Banshee.

　　Dr. Feldworts writes: "Lady Katherine had infamously warned explorers of the karmic dangers of plundering the Americas for riches. Against her own sage advice, she found herself making the perilous ocean crossing to the Virginia Colony in search of something precious; her missing map-maker son, taken by privateers. Bereft at his loss, she vowed vengeance and disappeared into the sweeping fog on the moors, shouting *'A curse on treasure hunters! Thine greed will be thy doom!'* She then certainly called upon her extensive knowledge of the ethereal realm to transform herself into the avenging banshee."

Dr. Feldworts continues: "To this day, there are sunken shipwrecks from Florida to Maine overloaded with buried treasure that the Bollin Banshee fiercely watches over."

3.   Theories abound regarding the origin of the zombie cows; some say they were merely drunken beasts accustomed to binging on the fermented mash discharged from the distillery. Over the years, process improvements removed the inebriating effluent and the cows, once detoxed, returned to normal. And while scant historical documentation exists on the topic of bovine upending, this appears to be the first documented case of 19th century cow-tipping. What served as a clever escape for Dr. Thalmeus evolved into a pastoral pastime, a veritable rite-of-passage for college students.

4.   The famous sculptures and concrete objects found around Lake Anne Plaza were created by Uruguayan sculptor, Gonzolo Fonseca. Robert 'Bob' Simon said of Fonseca: "His charge was to design something the kids could climb on, to create humor we all could participate in."
From *In His Own Words: Stories from the Extraordinary Life of Reston's Founder, Robert E. Simon, Jr.*
—by Kristina S. Alcorn, Great Owl Books, 2016.

5.   The W&OD Trail was formerly the Washington & Old Dominion Railroad from 1859 until 1968, which ran through the heart of Reston, past the bourbon factory. "The Choochoocabra, while a terrifying animal, kept the railroad tracks free of livestock, eliminating disruptions en route service which allowed robust trade and economic flourishing of the region."
From *The Wild Life of Wildlife on the Olde W&OD*
—by Nordwood Harvington, Shenandoah Ink Publishers

EDITOR'S NOTE: There are far more myths to be researched as our work continues: The Wereduck, The Hovering Eyeball, Vampire Voles, Pirates Quay Hideaway, Marathon Medusa, Ginormo the Snapping Turtle, the Fairy Folk of Glade Stream Valley, Snake Den Demetria, the location of the Treasure of Eight Thousand Cursed Souls... just to name a few. We'll keep digging for the truth!

Thank You

The authors would like to thank the individuals and organizations who inspired us and made this work possible: Walker Nature Center, Reston Regional Library, Reston Museum, Reston Used Book Store, Goldstein & Guilliams PLC, and special thanks to You the Reader.

Note

This collection is protected under the copyright laws of the United States and other countries throughout the world. Country of first publication: United States of America. Any unauthorized exhibition, distribution, or copying of this book or any part thereof may result in civil liability and criminal prosecution. The story, all names, characters, and incidents portrayed in this collection are fictitious. No identification with actual persons, places, buildings, and products is intended or should be inferred.

The views and opinions expressed in this work do not necessarily reflect those of the authors, the research team, the publisher, or even those quoted as expressing such.

The authors are quite aware of the anachronisms and inconsistencies of Dr. Thalmeus' statements in his journal, and are currently looking into it.

No mythical animals or beings were harmed in regards to the making of this book.

PHOTOS: *All photo images used with permission, and thanks!*
By Caroline Schor-MacDicken
Cover: *Lake Anne Sunset*; Back cover: *Lake Anne Dusk*;
pii magnifying glass, p02 compass, p15 acorn, p19 cowbell,
p31 autumn leaf one, p33 autumn leaf two.
p03 Journal of Dr. Padraigin W. Thalmeus, PDS. by Dirk MacAbre

Eric MacDicken

Eric has ventured to Scotland on several occasions, and once when he was younger went swimming in Loch Ness. He didn't meet Nessie that day, but he did get a monstrous case of pneumonia. A writer, art director, designer, creative consultant, and illustrator, Eric has been featured in the *Graphic Artists Guild's Directory of Illustration*. He first moved to Reston in 1970, and lives there with his wife, enjoying the nature and wildlife of the area.

Kristina S. Alcorn

Kristina is the author of *In His Own Words: Stories from the Extraordinary Life of Reston's Founder, Robert E. Simon, Jr.* (Great Owl Books, 2016), a lifelong Restonian, photographer, and lover of a well-told story. She lives in Reston with her husband and children and a revolving cast of feline houseguests.

Eric's original pencil sketch for the Reckless Huntsman of Haunter's Woods

CPSIA information can be obtained at www.ICGtesting.com
Printed in the USA
BVIW12n1854121116
467623BV00001B/1

* 9 780099 7314137 *